Barbara Hepworth drawings from a sculptor's landscape

Barbara Hepworth

DRAWINGS FROM A SCULPTOR'S LANDSCAPE

with an Introduction to the drawings by **Alan Bowness**

FREDERICK A. PRAEGER, *Publishers*
New York · Washington

BOOKS THAT MATTER

Published in the United States of America in 1967
by Frederick A. Praeger, Inc., Publishers
111 Fourth Avenue, New York, N.Y. 10003

Library of Congress Catalog Card Number 67–13169
Printed in Great Britain

Square with two circles, 1963 (Churchill College, Cambridge)

contents

a sculptor's landscape

8

Haworth, Yorkshire

Cow and Calf rocks above Ilkley

I cannot write anything about landscape without writing about the human figure and human spirit inhabiting the landscape. For me, the whole art of sculpture is the fusion of these two elements—the balance of sensation and evocation of man in this universe. At an early age I began to observe the movements and behaviour of people, to study their posture and gestures and anticipate what was about to happen. Were people around me ill, or cross, or anxious? Why did the people in the asylum opposite shuffle along when they had green grass and trees, whereas we were so gay just playing on the paving-stones outside?

I think I must have been obsessive and secretive and obstinate from birth, and a difficult child to live with. I remember my first day at school and the fantastic sensuous joy of the smell of the paints I was given and the brilliance of the colours I used, and the terrible scene that ensued when the class ended, the paints were taken away and I screamed and screamed.

Then at the age of seven there was a lecture with slides on Egyptian sculpture given by the headmistress, who later became one of my greatest friends and helpers, and my mind was completely focused. This was the world I understood, and I must get to know more! So I read everything I could: I made models, did portraits in clay and plaster of my sisters, I rejected all the pictures around me and tried to find the contacts that would enable me to go orientated in the world that meant reality to me. More and more I observed the granite sets, the steep hills of industrial Yorkshire, the scurrying of mill girls in their shawls huddled against the cold and wind—the lonely figure against a street gas-lamp, the squatting miner outside his door, and the gleaming 'withinness' of his sparkling ugly house.

Then came the great day when I was allowed to go with my father on his rounds of roads and bridges, in the course of his duties as civil engineer. I became a sort of bird soaring over the landscape. My father would mention very quietly the stresses and strains of roads and bridges and we would then continue to float through the landscape in our private thoughts. It was an early and very high car, which enabled us to see over hedges. At the furious pace of about 25 miles per hour, and being very careful not to disturb the horses and drivers of their carts, we roamed through the dales and valleys and up the moors, and through the Pennines. From the deep indigo and black and scarlets of the industrial heart we sailed through unimaginable beauty of unspoiled countryside. The position of man in relation to this country, and the horror of the approaching slump and then the First World War, absorbed all my thoughts. The exploitation of man, the image of human dignity in spite of these horrors, obsessed me. I would imagine stone 'images' rising out of the ground, which would pinpoint the spiritual triumph of man and at the same time give the sensuous, evocative, and biologically necessary fetish for survival.

My father was an exceptional person. In all the years I knew and treasured his friendship I never once heard him be angry or say an unkind word. He never intruded on my thoughts and he was very silent, and so we travelled, in quiet harmony, through the industrial heart of the West Riding and through the superb country. These photographs which I have taken of Yorkshire were chosen nostalgically. The textures, the form and the sense of movement all belong to my sculptor's world, where you (the reader) and I the sculptor become one, and here we create an image that combines all our unspoken perceptions of infinite continuity of life and the physical apprehension of time and space.

At an early stage I became troubled about the 'graven image', but I decided that it was sin only when the image sought to elevate the pretensions of man instead of man praising God and his universe. Every work in sculpture is, and must be, an act of praise and an awareness of man in his landscape. It is either a figure I see, or a sensation I have, whether in Yorkshire, Cornwall or Greece, or the Mediterranean.

In spite of being such a silent and obstinate child, I must have been surrounded by real love and understanding. At home I was allowed to make an awful mess. At school I was allowed to paint and draw whenever I was free to do so. A strange kind of obstinacy made me do studies of my white mice, newts, and frogs, which never got me a prize, but made me highly critical. At a fairly early age I got hold of Thompson's book on Anatomy and studied it furiously. The wonderful structure of the human frame is an architecture of highest proportion, and all sensitivity to landscape is in one's ability to feel within one's body: to feel with a primitive humility a response to life and location, a response to form, texture and rhythm, and a response to the magic of light, both sun and moon everchanging. A great gift my parents gave me and my sisters and brother was the annual trip to Robin Hood's Bay. Here we stayed in a house on rock rising out of the beach. I had an attic room and would get up at dawn to go painting all by myself and undisturbed in a world of fantastic beauty. The rocky scars, the boats, sea and cliffs inspired me continuously. Artists lived in Robin Hood's Bay and I was able to go and sniff the smell of paint and canvas and explore this wonderful free world of changing light and tide and colour. These holidays must have started early in my life because the only prize I got at school was for a collection of seaweeds gathered from the pools at the age of seven. But here I painted and studied the structure of natural forces, and noticed the importance of a figure standing far out on the rocks.

I began to co-ordinate the human figure and landscape.

Near Keighley, Yorkshire

The artist sketching near St Ives

Many years later I moved into this Cornish landscape, where the superb light and colour emphasize the importance of man in landscape. Again many years, and I managed to get to Greece, where the same extraordinary thing happened. In that supreme light the importance of a human being in the landscape became predominant.

I have been in St Ives over a quarter of a century. Never, in the time, have I seen two days alike. Here I have found the same bones and roots and scars and tissues as in Yorkshire; but in addition there is light and warmth, and a sense of gaiety of movement that has left our great cities. Here I can slowly travel to a near-by hill and, with larks singing above and the distant sound of sea and wind and voices carrying from far-away farms, a distant figure is a monument, whilst I myself am cradled in the anatomy of landscape.

I rarely draw what I see—I draw what I feel in my body. Sculpture is a three-dimensional projection of primitive feeling: touch, texture, size and scale, hardness and warmth, evocation and compulsion to move, live, and love. Landscape is strong—it has bones and flesh and skin and hair. It has age and history and a principle behind its evolution.

I detest arbitrary form like an indented pillow or a misshapen potato. In all natural forces there is an underlying principle of growth and form, endlessly adjusting and purifying itself. Only when man intervenes, as in open-cast mining, does the landscape become as shapeless and ugly as an old pillow.

Whenever I am embraced by land and seascape I draw ideas for new sculptures: new forms to touch and walk round, new people to embrace, with an exactitude of form that those without sight can hold and realize. For me it is the same as the touch of a child in health, not in sickness. The feel of a loved person who is strong and fierce and not tired and bowed down. This is not an aesthetic doctrine, nor is it a mystical idea. It is essentially practical and passionate, and it is my whole life, as expressed in stone, marble, wood and bronze.

Delphi, theatre and temple of Apollo

Epidauros, the theatre

Mycenae

In Greece the inspiration was fantastic. I ran up the hills like a hare, with my notebook, to get there first and have the total impact of solitude. I made many drawings for new sculptures called Delphi, Delos, Mycenae, Epidauros, and Santorin. These forms were my experience there. After my solitude I waited for the 199 people I had left behind and watched their movements and responses on entering the architecture in the superb location of mountain, hill and plain. This was very anti-social, I admit; but I had waited thirty years to get to Greece.

To get up early and be the first to climb up to Santorin, to find my place at the top of the theatre of Epidauros, surrounded by the sighing wind above, and warmed by the worn marble—with the heavenly sound of the human voice coming from below and the whole vast and glorious shape below me—was the embodiment of the sculptor's landscape. Timeless and in space, pure in conception and like a rock to hold on to, these forms in Greece have been a constant source of inspiration—Patmos in particular, where the curve of the horizon was omnipotent and the islands rose up from the water like flowers in the sun. A sculptor's landscape embraces all things that grow and live and are articulate in principle: the shape of the buds already formed in autumn, the thrust and fury of spring growth, the adjustment of trees and rocks and human beings to the fierceness of winter—all these belong to the sculptor's world, as well as the supreme perception of man, woman and child of this expanding universe. It is within our bodies to feel and to be, and in making a sculpture we do, in fact, make a talisman that enables us to enter our architecture and look at our painting as fully posed human beings. Every movement we make has its meaning. And I have seen, as I have elsewhere written, people enter the Piazza San Marco in Venice with an entirely different physical bearing, reacting to the space and proportion around them, and I have seen wonderful teams in operating theatres work together with instinctive grace and harmony of movement, making a spontaneous composition of the highest order.

I usually get dancers as models and ask them to move about, to limber up, to relax and to move and move until I know them all the way round. I become the model and the drawing becomes me. But always it is the structure and spirit which is the inspiration.

I have included a photograph of St Ives taken for me from the air. For twenty-five years, walking through these streets, I have felt through my feet the geological shape of the place. The aerial view proved to me my point; it is through our senses that form, colour and meaning are given to everything we make and do. I wrote about St Ives many years ago: 'The sea, a flat diminishing plane, held within itself the capacity to radiate an infinitude of blues, greys, greens and even pinks of strange hues, the lighthouse and its strange rocky island was the eye: the Island of St Ives an arm, a hand, a face. The rock formation of the great

St Ives. The Artist's studio is in the centre foreground

Sea Form (Atlantic), 1964

bay had a withinness of form which led my imagination straight to the country of West Penwith behind me—although the visual thrust was straight out to sea. The incoming and receding tides made strange and wonderful calligraphy on the pale granite sand which sparkled with felspar and mica. The rich mineral deposits of Cornwall were apparent on the very surface of things; quartz, amethyst, and topaz; tin and copper below in the old mineshafts; geology and prehistory —a thousand facts induced a thousand fantasies of form and purpose, structure and life, which had gone into the making of what I saw and what I was.' I also wrote to Sir Herbert Read (*The Meaning of Art*): 'Working realistically replenishes one's *love* for life, humanity and the earth' (Here I would now add 'the universe').

Working abstractly seems to release one's personality and sharpen the perception so that in the observation of life it is the wholeness, or inner intention, that moves one so profoundly: the components fall into place, the detail is significant of unity.

When I start drawing and painting abstract forms I am really exploring new forms, hollows, and tensions which will lead me where I need to go. Planes and curves are the pure rhythm of stance and energy. The pierced hole allows bodily entry and re-entry. The spiral takes hold of one's hand and arm. A fullness can be a breast, or a head or a shoulder. A hollow can be the taut hollow in the thigh. Strings can twist one from the front to the back, and colour establish the mood of place and time. Out of all these components I search for new associations of form and hollow and space, and a new tautness and awareness for the growth of new sculptures.

Pelagos, 1946

Sculpture is to me an affirmative statement of our will to live: whether it be small, to rest in the hand; or larger, to be embraced; or larger still, to force us to move around it and establish our rhythm of life. Sculpture is, in the twentieth century, a wide field of experience, with many facets of symbol and material and individual calligraphy. But in all these varied and exciting extensions of our experience we always come back to the fact that we are human beings of such and such a size, biologically the same as primitive man, and that it is through drawing and observing, or observing and drawing, that we equate our bodies with our landscape. A sculptor's landscape is one of ever-changing space and light where forms reveal themselves in new aspects as the sun rises and sets, and the moon comes up. It is a primitive world; but a world of infinite subtle meaning. Nothing we ever touch and feel, or see and love, is ever lost to us. From birth to old age it is retained like the warmth of rocks, the coolness of grass and the ever-flow of the sea.

St Ives, April 1966

the drawings of Barbara Hepworth

ALAN BOWNESS

Over the past hundred years we have slowly come to appreciate the character and significance of the sculpture of painters. Degas, Renoir, Gauguin, Matisse, Picasso and others have all shown what a painter can contribute to the art of sculpture, and sculptors themselves are the first to acknowledge their debt. We realize that this is a special sort of sculpture, distinguished in kind from sculptor's sculpture—and one can analyse how—but none the worse for that.

The paintings of sculptors, on the other hand, remain—Giacometti apart—in a critical limbo, with few people knowing quite what to think about them. Rodin, Brancusi, Gabo, Moore, and Hepworth, to take five obvious names, are between them responsible for a considerable number of drawings and paintings of unusual interest. With some exceptions, however, this work is rarely exhibited or reproduced, and it is largely unstudied and neglected. This book is an attempt to do justice to one of the five, Barbara Hepworth, and this introduction a suggestion of how such work should be regarded.

One can understand the difficulties, and also admit that sculptors' paintings are of less general consequence for the art of our time than the painters' sculptures. There are good reasons for this: the most obvious being that they are far fewer in number, largely because there are many fewer sculptors than painters. They have in consequence never won the stature that painters' sculpture has won, and this prestige can in itself encourage the activity—so much so that most painters have felt the impulse to try their hand at sculpture, often with very interesting results.

A sculptor's paintings also suffer from certain disadvantages, which they inevitably share with a painter's sculpture: for example, discontinuity, by which I mean that the work does not fall into a regular and logical progression, but proceeds in fits and starts, with long pauses and sometimes apparently self-contained groupings. Such work is in any case always tangential to the artist's first art, something that does not occupy him regularly and permanently, but to which he turns on occasion, perhaps in order to approach a problem from another direction, or perhaps to give him a release from obsessions that have grown too pressing. In some ways, of course, this is not, in fact, a disadvantage: on the contrary, but it makes the nature of the activity a rather special one, and direct comparisons between a painter's paintings and a sculptor's paintings can be misleading and unhelpful.

And then, for the sculptor, drawing and painting can fulfil several roles. First and most obviously comes drawing from the figure, an indispensable activity for the sculptor, because his art is homocentric—related to images of ourselves—in a way the painter's more illusionistic art is not. But a sculptor's life drawings are unlike a painter's—he is looking at the figure with, consciously or unconsciously, different things in mind. At the student stage, it is obviously a question of three-dimensional representation of the figure which must concern him. The translation into sculptural form of the form of the body must be understood by any sculptor, because anything he does later, however abstract, is certain to reflect on this relationship, so fundamental is it to our appreciation of sculpture.

Beyond this kind of figure drawing the sculptor enters into a world of almost irresponsible freedom. His paintings and drawings are often uninhibited in a way that the painter's work is not. They can be more truly experimental, though at the time the work may seem to be a little out of touch with main issues. In fact, it may be concerned with certain problems that are not central to painters' interests at the time they are done, but which may nevertheless be of considerable long-term significance for the development of painting. To take an example: rhythm matters little to most painters today: it is an extremely important part of most sculptors' drawings, Barbara Hepworth's in particular.

More important, though, is the way a sculptor uses drawing and painting as a means of generating sculptural ideas. The relevance of a sculptor's drawings may not at first be obvious: sometimes they may appear to be so many decorative exercises, but as one studies them in relation to the artist's sculpture their purpose and function become clear.

One can see this the moment one looks at the drawings and paintings reproduced in this book. The earliest (plates 1 and 2) are included as characteristic examples fo a kind of life drawing practised by Barbara Hepworth as a very young sculptor. There were many hundreds of these, some of them rapid three-minute studies of a pose, others more deeply considered to ask (as those illustrated do) what must happen as the idea is translated into sculpture. The forms take on a greater amplitude; they become less personal and individualized and more universal and abstract. These are the qualities of the sculpture of this period—for example, the *Contemplative Figure*, carved in Polyphant Stone in 1928 (fig. 1). Between sculpture and drawings there is a direct relationship: both share an evident mastery of conventional techniques, as though the young artist takes pleasure in demonstrating her accomplishments. This is, of course, more marked in the sculpture, where already the quality of the carving is exceptional, but it is equally true of the drawings with their mixed use of ink, crayon, charcoal, and wash.

In these very early drawings the sculptor's own personality is still somewhat muted. They invite comparison with the better-known figure drawings of Henry

Fig

Moore done in the late 1920's. There are common influences at work, a way of drawing from life that was widely accepted in England in the 1920's (compare, for example, Dobson's or Skeaping's early drawings) and, of more fundamental importance, the figure style of the early Italian Renaissance. Both Moore and Hepworth studied this when they were in Italy. 'I explored the whole of Tuscany's Romanesque architecture in landscape and sunlight; Masaccio; Michelangelo; Cimabue; Giotto; Assissi; Siena, and Perugia'—this is how Barbara Hepworth describes the year she spent in Italy after leaving the Royal College of Art in 1924, and the four artists she names are particularly relevant.

Very few drawings of the 1920's have survived; they were for the most part properly regarded as expendable studies, and no particular regard was set upon them. The same general observation is true of the drawings of the 1930's—only a handful are known and recorded, and although many of them are certainly lost, this was a period when the activity of drawing seemed to matter less to the sculptor.

One can understand why. The decade was of such importance to her creative development that to Barbara Hepworth carving must have seemed all-absorbing. As she says: 'In trying to find a new way of composing forms other than by the accepted order of human anatomy or by my own experience of the special forms induced by carving direct into the material, and feeling in harmony with the properties of wood or stone, I discovered a new approach which would allow me to build my own sculptural anatomy dictated only by my poetic demands from the material.'

This was the period of her marriage to Ben Nicholson, of their visits to France to see Brancusi, Arp, and Picasso, of continued friendship with Moore and Herbert Read, to the production of 'Circle' in 1937, of international exhibitions of 'constructive art', of close personal contact with Mondrian and Gabo. Of the later 1930's Barbara Hepworth has written: 'My own work went well. Carving became increasingly rhythmical and I was aware of the special pleasure which sculptors can have through carving, that of a complete unity of physical and mental rhythm. It seemed to be the most natural occupation in the world. It is perhaps strange that I should have become particularly aware of this at the moment when the forms themselves had become the absolute reversal of all that was arbitrary—when there had developed a deliberate conception of form and relationship.'

The kind of drawing associated with such sculptures as the *Pierced Hemisphere* of 1938 (fig. 2) is precise, measured, cool, and totally abstract—an examination of crystal structure and a construction of forms within cubes and circles and polyhedrons which reminds one that Barbara Hepworth has always found friends among mathematicians and pure scientists. It was no accident that the physicist J. D. Bernal should have written an introduction for the catalogue of her 1937 London exhibition.

fig. 2

With the outbreak of war in September 1939 Barbara Hepworth and Ben Nicholson moved with their young family to St Ives in Cornwall. This put an end to carving for several years: the only sculptures done until 1943 were some small plaster maquettes for sculptures with colour. In these circumstances, drawing offered an outlet for suppressed creative imagination, as the artist herself makes clear: 'In the late evenings, and during the night, I did innumerable drawings in gouache and pencil—all of them abstract, and all of them my own way of exploring the particular tensions and relationships of form and colour which were to occupy me in sculpture during the later years of the war.'

These drawings of 1940–2 (plates 3–6) represent one of Barbara Hepworth's major achievements. They follow on from the occasional drawings of the 1930's, but go much further. Their starting-point is a regular form, sometimes quite simple and explicit, as with the globe of *Circle* (no. 6), or the ellipse of *Oval Form* (no. 4), but sometimes implied and more complex, as with the crystal structures of nos. 3 and 5. Within these forms the space is explored and opened out; the sculptor using strings and colour and a gradation of tones.

The originality and historical importance of these drawings (and of the plaster sculptures which accompanied them) has yet to be recognized. Their significance lies in the way that certain ideas about space and rhythm, usually associated with constructivism, were brought into the language of sculpture. Naum Gabo was living in St Ives at the time, and a fruitful creative interchange between friends was possible, each artist nourishing the other. The pierced hole through the sculpture had been a startling feature of Hepworth's sculpture in the 1930's: now we see the richness of meaning which that interior space can possess.

Fig. 3

The lines of the strings are there to emphasize tensions within forms, without occupying space themselves. The coloured areas are solid concentrations of pure colour: in the drawings they do not have sculptural shape, but act over a wider area than that which they physically occupy. One can see this if one compares the drawings with the contemporary sculptures, for example *Wave* of 1944 (fig. 3). Instead of the sharp accents of red and blue that one finds in the drawings, here the entire interior is painted in the palest of blues. This colouring was in itself a major innovation, and its possibilities have been pursued in a long series of sculptures right up to the present day.

The ideas of the 1940–2 drawings were on the whole realized in the sculptures of the immediately succeeding years. This in its turn meant that the drawings went in search of new sculptural forms—instead of being enclosed within a circle or oval, the interior forms break out and dominate the exterior too. This is what happens in all the drawings of 1946–7 that are reproduced on plates 7 to 10. In particular, the spiral which coils out from the inside assumes a new importance (plate 7), and so do the rhythmic swinging arcs which generate a pattern of interlocking elliptical forms (plate 9). These in due course find a culmination in such sculptures as *Pendour* of 1947 (fig. 4) and *Helikon* of 1948 (fig. 5): the relationship of *Pendour* to such drawings as *Recumbent Form* (plate 10) is an

especially close one, and the drawing itself now much more clearly suggests a sculpture in a landscape than the earlier more analytical studies (e.g. plate 3) ever did. The technique has changed, too, with oil washes taking the place of gouache.

With the end of the war and of immediate postwar tensions comes a remarkable opening-out of Barbara Hepworth's work. This was as marked in drawing as in sculpture. From about 1947 onwards for several years different kinds of drawing exist together. Figure drawings take on a new importance and a new variety (plates 11–22); there is a major series of hospital studies executed in 1948–9 (plates 23–30); and the abstract drawings become more exploratory than ever (plates 31–36). As one would expect, the figurative and the abstract drawings are intimately related to one another and influence each other. The artist makes this clear in a long passage written about her work at this time:

Abstract drawing has always been for me a particularly exciting adventure. First there is only one's mood; then the surface takes one's mood in colour and texture; then a line or curve which, made with a pencil on the hard surface of many coats of oil or gouaches, has a particular kind of 'bite' rather like on slate; then one is lost in a new world of a thousand possibilities because the next line in association with the first will have a compulsion about it which will carry one forward into completely unknown territory. The conclusion will be reached only by an awareness of some special law of harmonics induced at the beginning with the second line to the first. Suddenly before one's eyes is a new form which, from the sculptor's point of view, free as it is from the problems of solid material, can be deepened or extended, twisted or flattened,

Fig. 5

19

Fig. 6

tightened and hardened according to one's will, as one imbues it with its own special life. The whole process is opposite to that of drawing from life.

With the model before one, every known factor has to be understood, filtered and selected; and then, from these elements in the living object, one chooses those which seem to be structurally essential to the abstract equivalent, relevant to the composition and material in which one wishes to convey the idea. After my exhibition in 1946 at Lefevre the abstract drawings which I did led me into new territory; the forms took on a more human aspect—forms separated as standing or reclining elements, or linked and pulled together as groups.

The earliest of the figure drawings were done at the end of 1947 and in 1948 (plates 13, 14, and 17). In each case we have two views of the same model, one subsidiary to the other. There is no suggestion of a fixed pose—which the artist dislikes intensely. She asks the model to move about naturally, pausing or resting at certain moments, but never taking up an artificial position. By preference she has used trained dancers on holiday, rather than professional artists' models. In the 1930's she had often watched dancers at work, and even drew ballet subjects, but as with Degas the interest was not in ballet as such, but in the nature of human movement.

The rhythm of the figure is expressed in the pencil line which describes the form. Some of the drawings are done on paper (for example, plates 11, 12*a*, 12*b*), but these tend to be the more summary ones. The more considered early ones are drawn on boards prepared with scumbled oil paints muted in colour; this is often scraped and rubbed off in places as the drawing proceeds. The pencil lines are strong and delicate, sometimes heightened with a coloured line—a red crayon, for example, in plate 17—and supported by softly shaded areas to bring out the forms. There is, however, no question of a three-dimensional realization of the figure, as there was in the very early figure drawings: the search is much more for the rhythm of a figure in movement. Profiles, for example, are important in giving a rhythmic pulse to the whole drawing.

This linear rhythmic quality is more pronounced in another group of figure studies, which were done in 1950 and 1951 (plates 16, 18–20, 22). There are no longer any shaded pencil passages, and the treatment of the figures is altogether simplified. The line is much freer: in the *Recumbent Figures—Blue* of October 1951, for example (plate 20), it does not even enclose the forms in places—a hint is enough. The style is chunkier, and although the forms are flatter and sometimes even silhouetted one feels that the sculptor is more aware of the sculptural relevance of these drawings than she was with the 1947–8 group. *Interlocking Forms* (plate 18) is very close to such sculptures of similar date as the Tate Gallery's *Bicentric Form* (fig. 6), and suggests inevitably two figures standing side by side.

The drawings are more populated, too—often with three figures (or three aspects of the same model, plates 15, 22), and sometimes more. This corres-

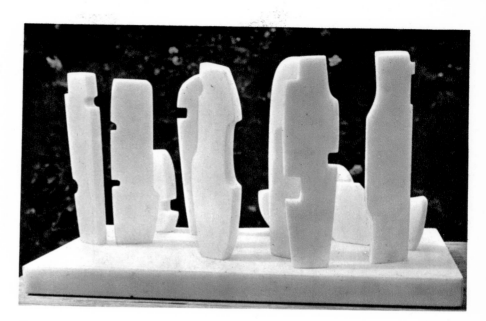

Fig. 7

ponds exactly with the concern for multiform sculptures, which reaches its cul-mination in the three *Groups* of 1951–2. *Group II* (*People Waiting*, fig. 7) might almost be regarded as the sculptural conclusion of the figure studies of 1950–1, for, despite the abstract nature of the forms, their human quality could hardly be more evident. It also reminds us that the distinction made between the figure studies and the abstract drawings of this period 1947–52 is an arbitrary one, for the *Women with Flags* of 1952 (plate 31) has also contributed to the *Groups*; so has, even more obviously, the *Drawings for Stone Sculpture* of 1947 (plate 33). This was one of the ideas for the L.C.C.'s abortive Waterloo Bridge competition, in which the sculptor sought an appropriate sculptural form for a place where a multitude of figures pass over and under the bridge. A social concern for people in communities is characteristic of Barbara Hepworth's work in the late 1940's, just as it is of Henry Moore's.

Another aspect of the interest in people at work comes in the remarkable series of operation-theatre studies which were done in 1948 and 1949 (plates 23–30). This is the most self-contained group of drawings in the artist's work, and the group that has least immediate sculptural application, though it is, of course, connected with the multifigure compositions of 1950–1 that have just been dis-cussed.

The theatre drawings have their origins in a characteristically human event —the serious illness of one of the artist's daughters, and a personal friendship that grew up with the surgeon who had operated on her. Knowing a sculptor's interest in anatomy and the structure of the body, he suggested that she might like to watch an operation taking place, and this Barbara Hepworth did first at the Princess Elizabeth Orthopaedic Hospital in Exeter and later in London at the National Orthopaedic Hospital and the London Clinic. She saw a number of very distinguished surgeons in action, performing complicated bone operations. She was allowed a pen and a sterilized pad to make notes, but the drawings were all done immediately afterwards with the scene retained in the artist's memory. In technique they are close to the figure paintings of 1947–8—drawn in pencil on a painted board, but much more use is made of colour—which is, of course, very abstract. The hospital drawings vary in subject from pictures of surgical teams at work (plates 24, 29) to studies of individual figures like the theatre sister (plates 25, 26). The most fascinating in many ways are the studies of hands (plates 27, 28): the manual delicacy and dexterity demanded of sculptor and surgeon are much more alike than one at first imagines.

Barbara Hepworth has herself given an account of what this meant to her in both human and artistic terms: this is so revealing that it warrants quotation:

Fig. 8

. . . when, in about the middle of 1947, a suggestion was made to me that I might watch an operation in a hospital, I expected that I should dislike it; but from the moment when I entered the operating theatre I became completely absorbed by two things: first, the extraordinary beauty of purpose and co-ordination between human beings all dedicated to the saving of life, and the way that unity of idea and purpose dictated a perfection of concentration, movement, and gesture; and secondly by the way this special grace (grace of mind and body) induced a spontaneous space composition, an articulated and animated kind of abstract sculpture very close to what I had been seeking in my own work.

We are all conditioned to seeing the nerveless kind of scurrying movement of modern life: dressed often in absurd clothes and with tense faces, blind to all but the necessity of working one's way through the crowds, we fight our way through the days and weeks. When we need refreshment, most people seek the nourishment of graceful movement in watching football matches, the ballet, horse-racing, or Wimbledon. But our participation is at second or third hand; we forget, or we have no time in which to remember, that grace of living can only come out of some kind of training or dedication, and that to produce a culture we have to understand all the attributes of a proper co-ordination between hand and spirit in our daily life. A particularly beautiful example of the difference between physical and spiritual animation can be observed in a delicate operation on the human hand by a great surgeon. The anatomy of the unconscious hand exposed and manipulated by the conscious hand with the scalpel, expresses vividly the creative inspiration of superb co-ordination in contrast to the unconscious mechanism. The basic tenderness of the large and small form, or mother and child, proclaims a rhythm of composition which is in contrast to the slapping and pushing of tired mother and frustrated child through faults in our way of living and unresolved social conditions.

For two years I drew, not only in the operating theatres of hospitals, but from groups in my studio and groups observed around me. I studied all the changes and defects which occurred in the composition of human figures when there were faulty surroundings or muddled purpose. This led me to renewed study of anatomy and structure as well as the structure of integrated groups of two or more figures. I began to consider a group of separate figures as a single sculptural entity, and I started working on the idea of two or more figures as a unity, blended into one carved and rhythmic form. Many subsequent carvings were on this theme, for instance Bicentric Form *in the Tate Gallery* (fig. 6).

In the mid-1950's drawing becomes a less important activity again. This is the period of the journey to Greece in 1954, and the magnificent monumental wood carvings with Greek names—Corinthos, Delphi, Delos—that were created immediately afterwards. They represent such a definitive statement of the carver's art that in a way it is hardly surprising to find them followed by one of the most radical departures in Barbara Hepworth's development. For in 1956 began the experiments with metal sculpture, first cut and twisted sheets of copper and brass, and then the use of bronze itself.

These new materials demanded new forms and subtle modifications of familiar ones. Here the drawings played a vital role in the explorations that were necessary. One has only to consider an early sheet-metal sculpture like *Orpheus* (fig. 8) of 1956 in conjunction with drawings of the same year (e.g. plates 38, 40) to appreciate this. *Orpheus* might, in fact, be said to be closer to the earlier drawings in that it lacks any solid form and echoes in its perfectly regular curves the implied shapes of the strings. The drawings themselves were growing more free, and escaping the tight control that had once been so typical. The coloured grounds were no longer so discreet, but now began to break into the drawn form itself, as indeed in the drawings called *Orpheus* (plate 40) or in *Stringed Figure* (plate 39).

In the summer of 1957 this informality reached an unprecedented point: drawings like *Figures* (*Summer*, plate 41) and *Wind Movement* (plate 42) seemed at the time almost totally unrelated to everything that had gone before, and a contradiction of much that the artist stood for. Their meaning did not become clear until the ideas were translated into such bronze sculptures as *Meridian* of 1958 (fig. 9): then one appreciated that they were an important part of the search for forms natural to the bronze medium. Unlike carved sculpture, this can assume a much less regular shape, and Barbara Hepworth was very quick to see what was possible. Her way of working bronze retains the carver's rather than the modeller's approach, but she needed to know what kind of structures were possible and what forms molten metal would take.

The new freedom of the 1957 drawings was quickly absorbed into the general drawing style, and no startling new developments have occurred in the 1960's. What has most notably happened is that the drawings have become much larger

Fig. 9

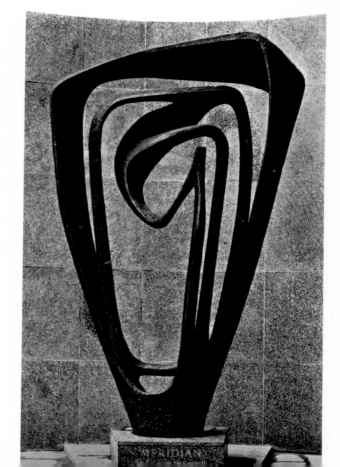

Fig. 11

Fig. 10

Fig. 12

Fig. 13

Fig. 14

and grander in scale, and altogether more painterly, with colour playing an increasingly dominant role. They might more properly be called paintings. The boards are prepared as before with scumbled oil paint, making rich and variegated textures on which accents of stronger colour and thicker paint are placed. Of late the paint has tended to be more liquid, and sometimes already establishes the form which the drawn pencil line does little more than confirm (as, for example, in *Genesis II*, plate 72). But it is the tightness and precision of the pencil line which attract attention. This is at once suggestive of sculptural form, and yet is also mysterious in a celestial way—it is no accident that words referring to sea and sky should so often appear in the titles.

Certain general directions are clear enough. There is a continued interest in multiple forms, as in the *Forms in Echelon* (plates 65, 67), which have their parallels in many recent multi-part sculptures, for example *Two Forms* (*Gemini*, fig. 12). Most of the forms remain oval, like the aperture of *Totem* (fig. 10), of the large marble *Pierced Form* (fig. 11), with its subtle curved lines. On the other hand, the idea of sculpture made from flat slabs, rectilinear in form, pierced with perfect circles, has also been an attractive one. It has been adumbrated in drawings (plates 58, 60; also 70, 74, 76) and then leads on to such inventions as *Marble with Colour: Crete* (fig. 13) and the bronze *Square with Two Circles* (facing p. 5). These entirely regular forms occur in the Maquettes for large sculptures which were made early in 1966 (e.g. fig. 14), and they are now finding their ultimate expression in large-scale works.

Many of the drawings of the 1960's were made within view of the sea, in a studio overlooking the Atlantic beach of Porthmeor, and the movement of tides and the forms of waves and wave patterns on the sea-shore sometimes provide their immediate inspiration (plates 56, 63, 69, etc.). Shells are also important (plate 62): they show the same principles of growth that one can find in both crystal structure and the frame of the human body—they are all forms subject to the same natural laws, and sculpture for Barbara Hepworth must be in an analogous position. There is always this sure sense of the fitting, a confidence about the appropriate place of things, that runs right through her work. As her own writing elsewhere in this volume makes clear, she has always understood sculpture as being a celebration of figures in a landscape. 'Every work of sculpture is, and must be, an act of praise, an awareness of man in his landscape. Every drawing and painting by a sculptor is an exploration into the potential force of volume and space in relation to man in his landscape.'

biographical notes

Barbara Hepworth, D.B.E., daughter of H. R. Hepworth, C.B.E., and Gertrude A. Hepworth. Born at Wakefield, Yorkshire, England, 10 January 1903.

Educated at Leeds School of Art; Royal College of Art, London; Florence and Rome.

She has been married twice and has triplet children, a son and two daughters, born in 1934, by her second marriage to Ben Nicholson (marriage dissolved 1951). She lived and worked in London until 1939, and since then has lived in St Ives, Cornwall, where her studio and workshops are now situated.

Awards

1953	Second Prize in the International Sculpture Competition on the theme of 'The Unknown Political Prisoner'
1958	Created C.B.E. (Commander of the Order of the British Empire)
1959	'The Grand Prix' at the 5th Sao Paulo Biennale
1960	Honorary Degree (Hon. D.Litt.) University of Birmingham
1961	Honorary Degree (Hon. D.Litt.) University of Leeds
1963	'The Foreign Minister's Award' at the 7th Biennale, Tokyo
1965	Created D.B.E. (Dame Commander of the Order of the British Empire)
1966	Honorary Degree (Hon. D.Litt.) University of Exeter

Selected list of exhibitions and important commissions

1928	First exhibited in London
1931	Member of '7 & 5' Group, London
1933	Member of 'Abstraction-Creation', Paris Member of 'Unit One', London
1933–54	London, Lefevre Gallery
1949	New York, Durlacher Bros.
1950	Venice, 25th Biennale Retrospective exhibition of sculpture and drawings
1951	London, Two large sculptures for the Festival of Britain
1954	London, Whitechapel Art Gallery Retrospective exhibition of work from 1927 to 1954
1955	Retrospective exhibition touring art museums in the U.S.A. (1955–7)
1956–66	London, Gimpel Fils New sculpture
1958	Brussels, 'Fifty Years of Modern Art'
1959	Sao Paulo, 5th Biennale Retrospective exhibition
1960	Travelling retrospective exhibition: Montevideo, Comision Nacional de Belles Artes Buenos Aires, Museo Nacional de Belles Artes Santiago, Museo de Arte Contemporaneo Caracas, Museo de Belles Artes
1961	British Council travelling exhibition (Commonwealth) Antwerp, 6th Biennale, Middelheimpark Paris, Musée Rodin, International Exhibition of Sculpture

1962	London, Whitechapel Art Gallery Retrospective exhibition of sculpture of the last decade Keukenhof and Breda, Netherlands Art Foundation Exhibition of sculpture New York, Solomon R. Guggenheim Museum; 'Modern Sculpture from the Joseph Hirshhorn Collection'
1963	Tokyo, 7th Biennale
1964	Bochum, Germany, Stadtische Kunstgalerie: 'Contemporary English Art' London, Tate Gallery: 'Painting and Sculpture of a Decade' British Council travelling exhibition in Scandinavia 1964–5 'Barbara Hepworth'
1965	London, Tate Gallery: 'British Sculpture in the Sixties' Otterlo, Holland; Rijksmuseum Kröller-Müller: Retrospective exhibition, subsequently at Basle and Turin New York, Marlborough-Gerson Gallery: 'The English Eye'
1966	Karlsruhe, Germany: Retrospective exhibition Marlborough-Gerson Gallery, New York: One-man exhibition Essen, Germany: Retrospective Exhibition

Selected list of museums and public collections with works by Barbara Hepworth

Great Britain

London, Arts Council of Great Britain
London, British Council
London, London County Councils
London, Peter Stuyvesant Foundation
London, Tate Gallery
London, Victoria and Albert Museum
Aberdeen, Art Gallery and Industrial Museum
Birmingham, City Museum and Art Gallery
Bristol, City Art Gallery and Museum
Cornwall, County Council
Harlow, Harlow Borough Council
Ferens Art Gallery, Kingston-upon-Hull
Leeds, City Art Gallery
Manchester, City Art Gallery
Oxford, New College
Oxford, St Catherine's College
St Ives, Borough Council
Edinburgh, Scottish National Gallery of Modern Art
Swansea, The Glynn Vivian Art Gallery
Wakefield, City Museum and Art Gallery

Australia

Melbourne, National Gallery of Victoria
Perth, Western Australian Art Gallery
Sydney, National Gallery of New South Wales

Belgium

Antwerp, Middelheimpark

Brazil

Sao Paulo, Museu de Arte Modera de Sao Paulo
Valparaiso, Museum of Fine Arts

Canada

Ottawa, National Gallery of Canada
Vancouver, Vancouver Art Gallery
Toronto, The Art Gallery of Toronto

Germany

Duisburg, Wilhelm-Lehmbruck-Museum
Leverkusen, Stadtisches Museum

Holland

Otterlo, Rijksmuseum Kröller-Müller
Den Haag, Gemeentemuseum
Rotterdam, de Doelen Concert Hall

New Zealand

National Gallery of New Zealand
City of Auckland Art Gallery
Wairarapa Fine Arts Promotion Com. Masterton

U.S.A.

Buffalo, New York, Albright Art Gallery
Dallas, Museum of Fine Arts
Detroit, Institute of Arts
Minneapolis, Walker Art Center
Nebraska, University Art Gallery
Newhaven, Conn., Yale University Museum
New York, Museum of Modern Art
New York, United Nations
Northampton, Mass., Smith College Museum
St Louis, Missouri, Washingon University (Steinberg Hall)
Syracuse, Everson Museum of Art

Scandanavia

Sweden: Backakra, Dag Hammarskjöld Museum
Denmark: Kopenhagen, Carlsberg Foundation
Finland: Helsinki, The Marie-Louise and Gunnar Didrichsen Art Foundation

Important Commissions

1951	London, Festival of Britain, 'Turning forms' Arts Council of Great Britain, 'Contrapuntal forms' Hatfield, Technical College, England, 'Vertical forms'
1954	London, Royal Festival Hall, 'Monolith (Empyrean)'
1956	London, Mullard House, 'Theme on Electronics'
1958–9	London, State House, 'Meridian' (bronze)
1962	London, John Lewis Partnership, 'Winged figure' (aluminium)
1963	Chesterfield, Chetwynd House, 'Curved Reclining form (Rosewall)'
1963	New York, United Nations, 'Single form' (bronze) Dag Hammarskjöld Memorial, donated by the Jacob and Hilda Blaustein Foundation

Monographs

Gibson, William
'Barbara Hepworth', *Ariel Series*, Faber & Faber, London, 1946

Read, Sir Herbert (with a foreword by the artist)
Barbara Hepworth, Carvings and Drawings, Lund Humphries Ltd.,
London, 1952

Hammacher, Professor A. M.
'Barbara Hepworth', *Modern Sculpture Series*, A. Zwemmer,
London, 1958

Hodin, Dr J. P.
Barbara Hepworth, Life and Work, Lund Humphries Ltd., London, 1961

Shepherd, Michael
'Barbara Hepworth', *Art in Progress* Series, Methuen Ltd., London, 1963

the drawings

list of plates

56 Wave, 1963. Oil and pencil (19¾ × 23¾ in.) Joseph Hirschhorn, USA

57 Two circles, 1963. Oil and pencil (25 × 15 in.) Private collection

58 Three monoliths, 1964. Oil and pencil (19 × 26 in.) The late Helen Sutherland

59 Atlantic form (blue), 1963. Oil and pencil (25 × 18 in.) T. S. Stallabrass

60 Square forms 2 (green and ochre). Oil and pencil (36 × 18¼ in.) Jan de Graaf, USA

61 Goonhilly (September), 1963. Oil and pencil (18 × 24 in.) The artist

62 Shell form, 1963. Oil and pencil (26 × 20 in.) Mr and Mrs H. Mortimer

63 Porthmeor, 1963. Oil and pencil (18 × 24 in.) Private collection, Switzerland

64 Marble form, 1964. Oil and pencil (31¼ × 20¼ in.) Sir Kenneth Anderson

65 Forms in echelon (green), 1963. Oil and pencil (15 × 26¾ in.) Bryan Urquhart, USA

66 Night sky (Porthmeor), 1964. Oil and pencil (28 × 23¾ in.) The Lady Patricia Ramsay

67 Forms in echelon on an orange ground. Oil and pencil (18 × 22 in.) Mrs Seligman

68 Drawing for pierced form (May). Oil and pencil (30 × 40¾ in.) Mr and Mrs J. Pethybridge

69 Wave forms (Atlantic), 1964. (30 × 40 in.) Private collection

70 Construction 1, 1965. Oil and pencil (35 × 40 in.) The artist

71 Stringed figure, 1965. Oil and pencil (30 × 24 in.) Mrs K. B. Austin

72 Genesis II, 1966. Oil and pencil (26 × 26 in.) The artist

73 Wood form (Gothic), 1966. Oil and pencil (30 × 20 in.) The artist

74 Construction II, 1966. Oil and pencil (40 × 35 in.) The artist

75 Garden sculpture (marble), 1966. Oil and pencil (30 × 20 in.) The artist

76 Square form I, 1966. Oil and pencil (36 × 18 in.) The artist

Acknowledgements

The artist and publishers wish to thank the following for their help in the preparation of this book: Messrs Gimpel Fils Ltd, Marlborough Fine Art Ltd and Studio St Ives Ltd.

1 *Standing girl*, 1928 (17½ × 10¾ in.)

2 *Seated girl*, 1928 (14 × 8¾ in.)

3 *Drawing* (*crystal*), 1940 (12¾ × 13⅞ in.)

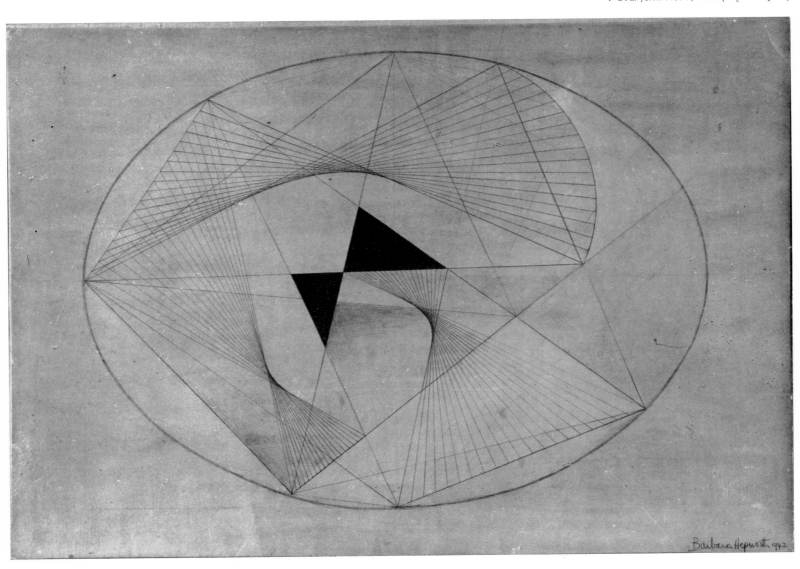

5 *Crystal*, 1942 (13 × 15 in.)

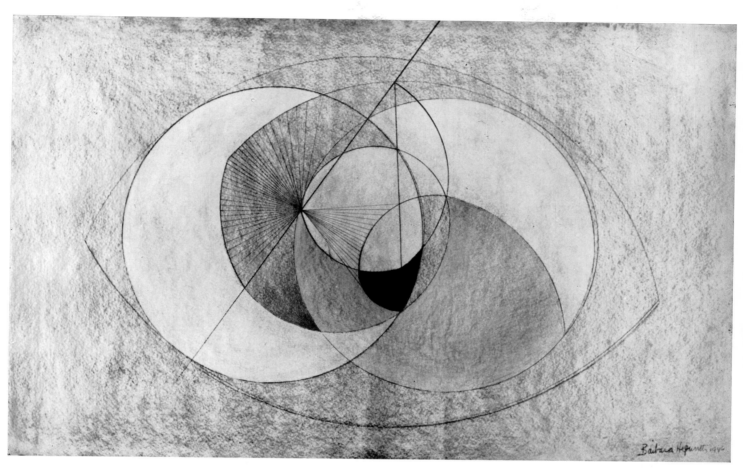

7 *Spiral with red*, 1946 (11⅜ × 19¾ in.)

6 *Circle*, 1942 (15 × 20¼ in.)

8 *Curved forms with red and yellow,* 1946 (10½ × 14¾ in.)

10 *Recumbent form, green and yellow*, 1947 (20 × 22 in.)

11 *Crouching figure,* 1949 (13¾ × 9¾ in.)

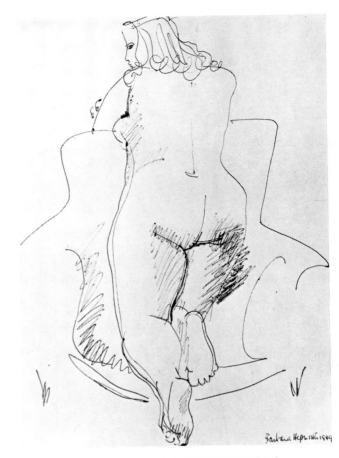

12a *Kneeling woman in armchair*, 1949 (14¾ × 10¼ in.)

12b *Woman in armchair*, 1949 (14¾ × 10¼ in.)

13 *Seated nude*, 1947 (11½ × 9 in.)

14 *Two figures with folded arms*, 1947 (14 × 10 in.)

15 *Group of three figures*, *Indian Red*, 1951 (20⅝ × 15½ in.)

Barbara Hepworth 1951

16 *Group of four figures—seascape* ($15\frac{1}{8} \times 18\frac{1}{4}$ in.)

17 *Girl with folded arms*, 1948 (16 × 12 in.)

19 *Three reclining figures (Prussian blue)*, (13 × 20⅝ in.)

20 *Recumbent figures — blue*, 1951 (23¾ × 16¾ in.)

21 *Lisa holding teacup* (*coin*), 1949 (12 × 16 in.)

22 *Group* (*three views of a young girl*), 1950 (18 × 14 in.)

Skiagram, 1949 (21½ × 14¼ in.)

24 *The scalpel*, 1948 (15 × 21 in.)

25 *Theatre Sister*, 1948 (13¼ × 9½ in.)

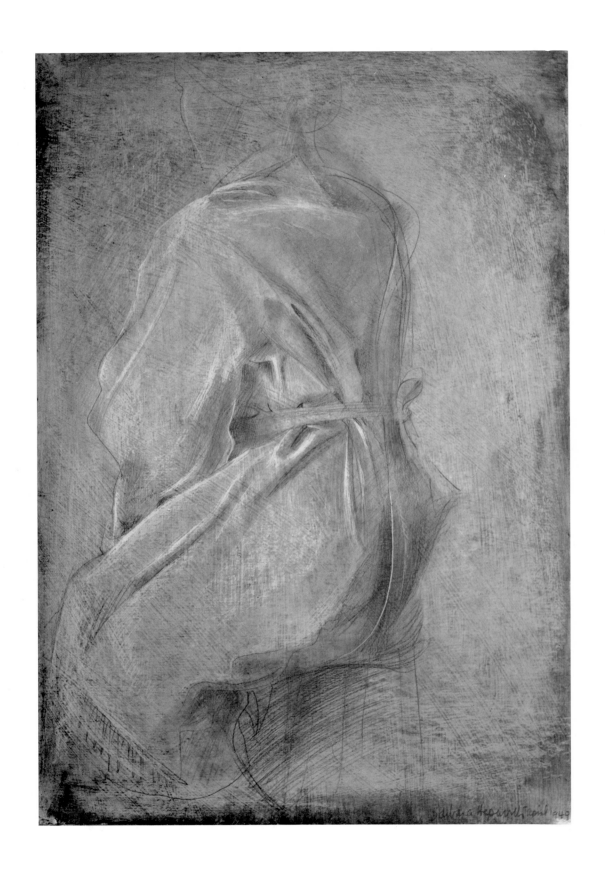

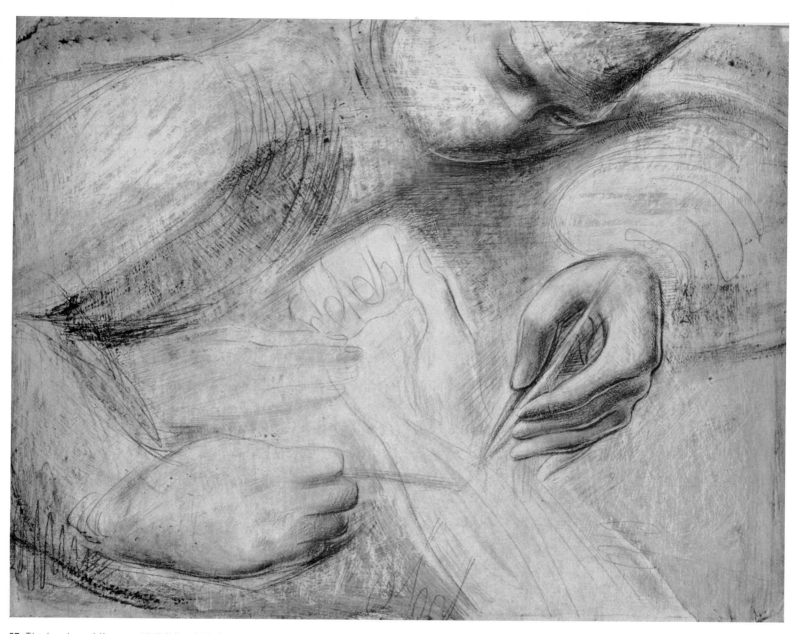

27 *The hands and the arm*, 1948 (12 × 15 in.)

26 *Theatre Sister* (*study of drapery*), 1949 (18 × 12 in.)

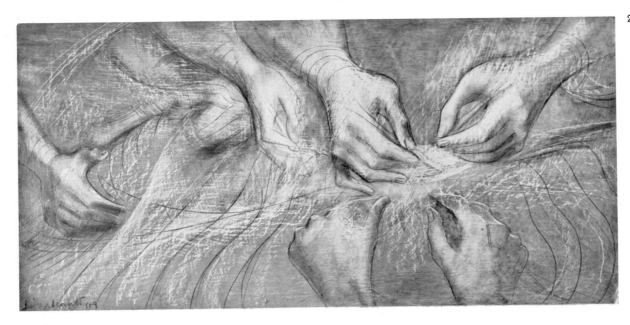

28 *Hands operating*, 1949 (10$\frac{1}{2}$ × 21 in.)

29 *Preparation*, 1949 (14$\frac{1}{2}$ × 20 in.)

30 *Concentration of hands No. 1*, 1948

32 *Green reclining form*, 1947 (11 × 15 in.)

31 *Women with flags*, 1952 (11¾ × 9¼ in.)

33 *Drawing for stone sculpture*, 1947 (13 × 25 in.)

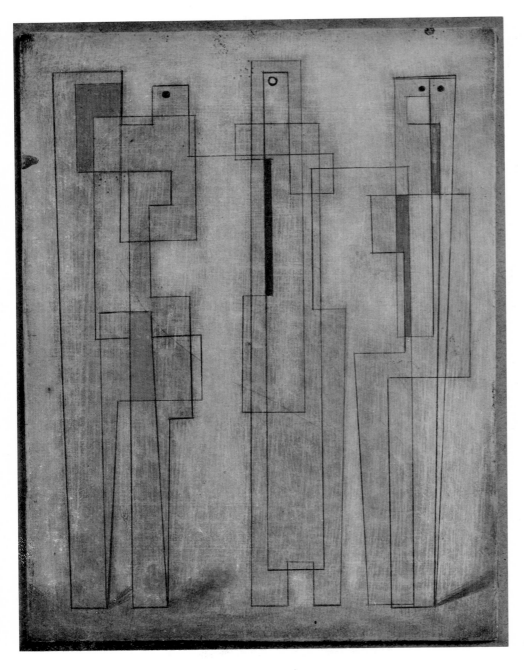

34 *Group with child (violet and red on brown)*, 1952 (11½ × 8¾ in.)

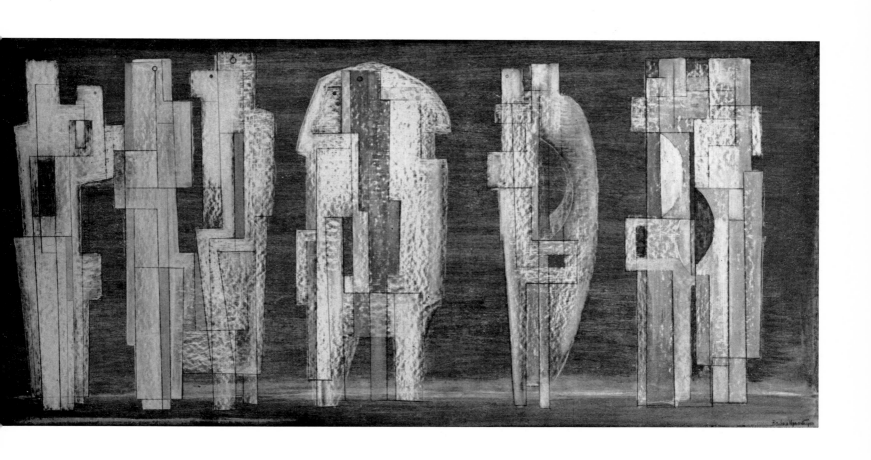

5 *Monolith—Pavan*, 1953 (24 × 28 in.)

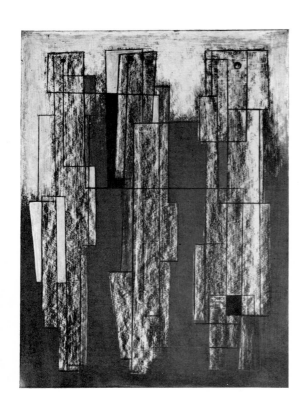

36 *Granite forms*, *red yellow and deep blue*, 1953 (14 × 10 in.)

37 *Curved forms—white and brown* (*Mycenae*), (17 × 15 in.)

38 *Rock form* (*Penwith*), 1956 (20 × 20 in.)

39 *Stringed figure,* 1956 (16 × 12 in.)

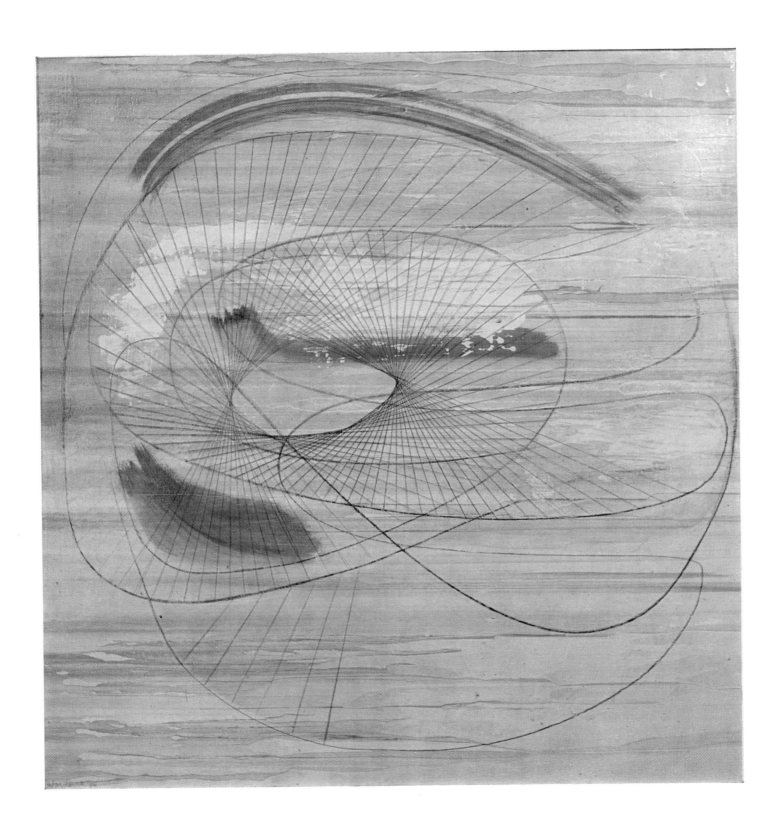

40 *Curved form* (*Orpheus*), 1956 (30 × 28 in.)

41 *Figures* (*summer*) *yellow and white*, 1957 (18¾ × 14 in.)

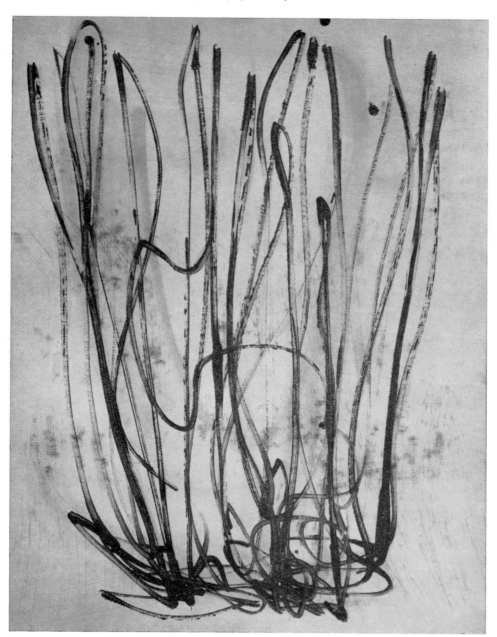

43 *Ascending form* (*monastral blue*), 1960 (24 × 11½ in.)

42 *Wind Movement No. 2*, 1957 (10 × 14½ in.)

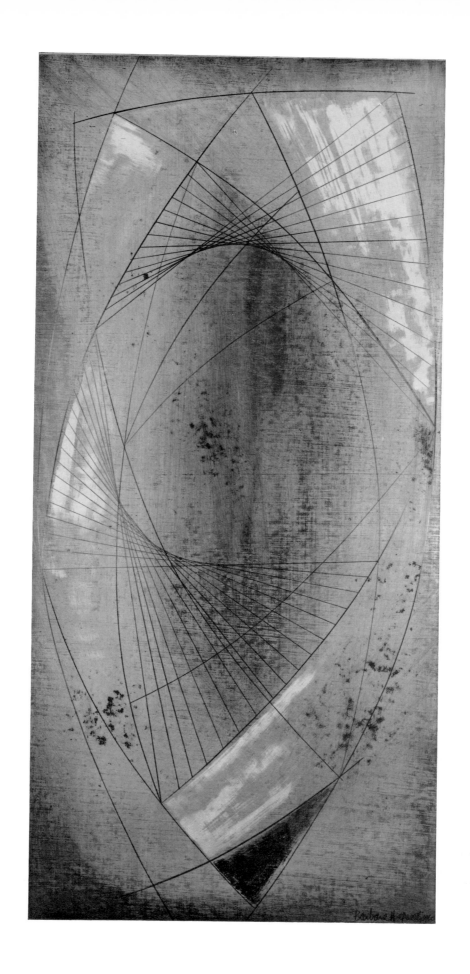

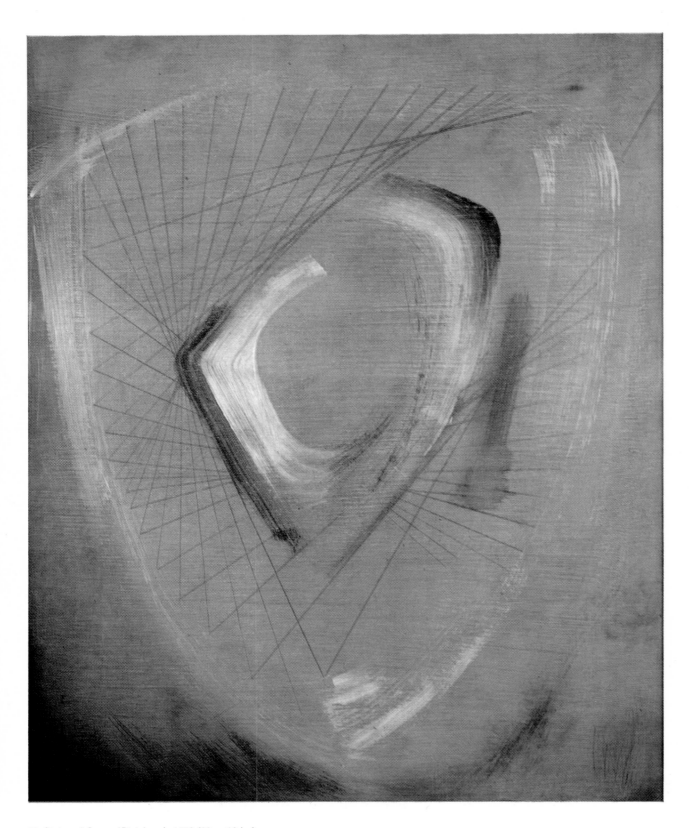

44 *Stringed figure* (*Finisterre*), 1956 (20 × 16 in.)

45 *Chios*, 1958 (20 × 14 in.)

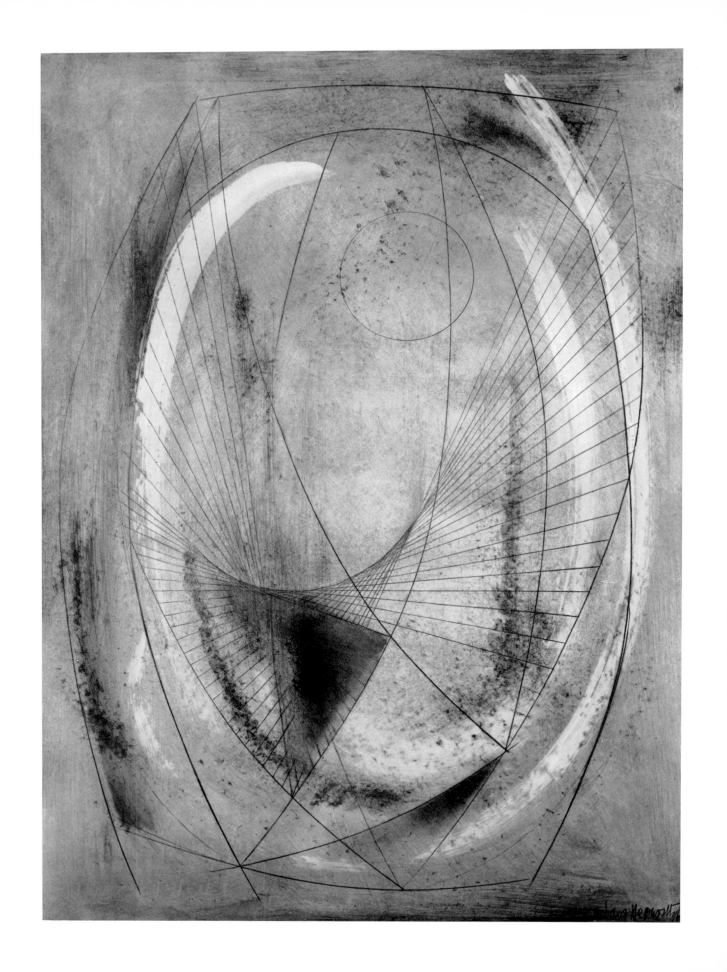

46 *Curved form* (*Porthmeor*), 1960 (25 × 18¼ in.)

47 *Rock forms*, 1961 (23⅜ × 12 in.)

48 *Stone form* (*Tresco*), 1961 (13 × 22 in.)   **49** *Stone form* (*Mincarlo*), 1961 (21¾ × 21 in.)

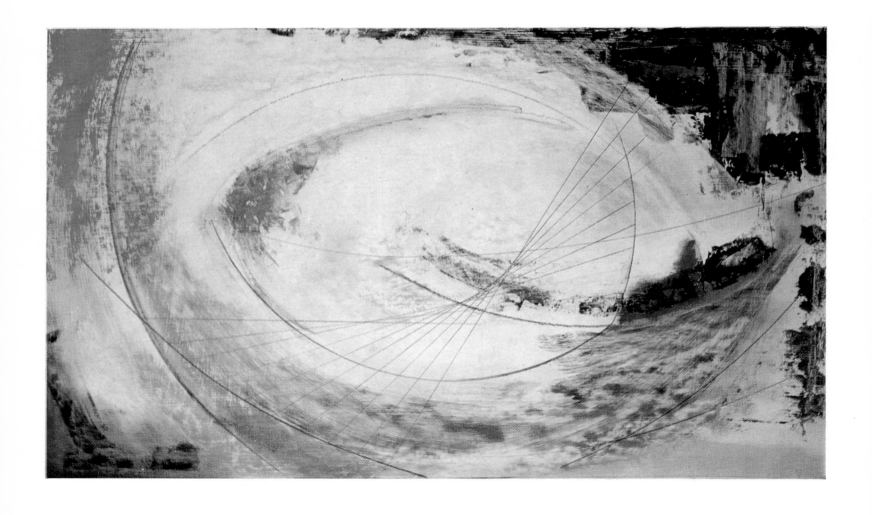

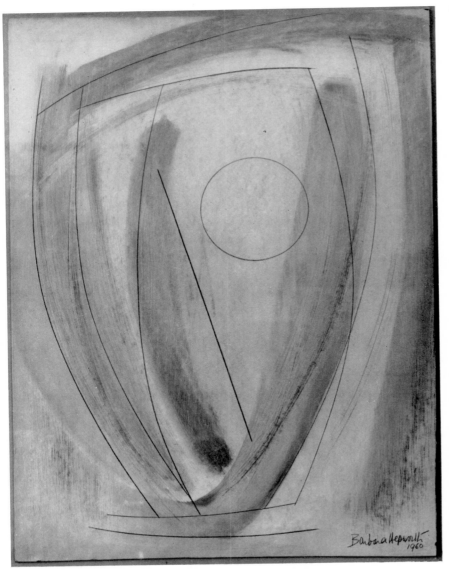

50 *Thea* (*incised form*), 1960 (24 × 18 in.)

51 *Incised form* (*granite*), 1960 (19½ × 16 in.)

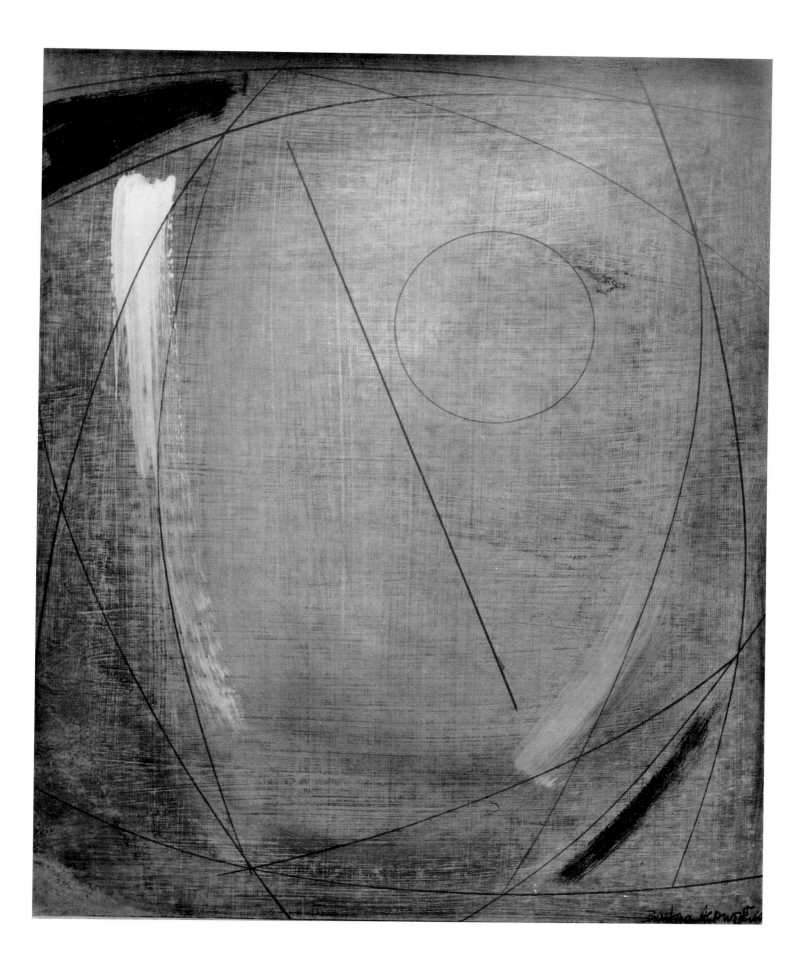

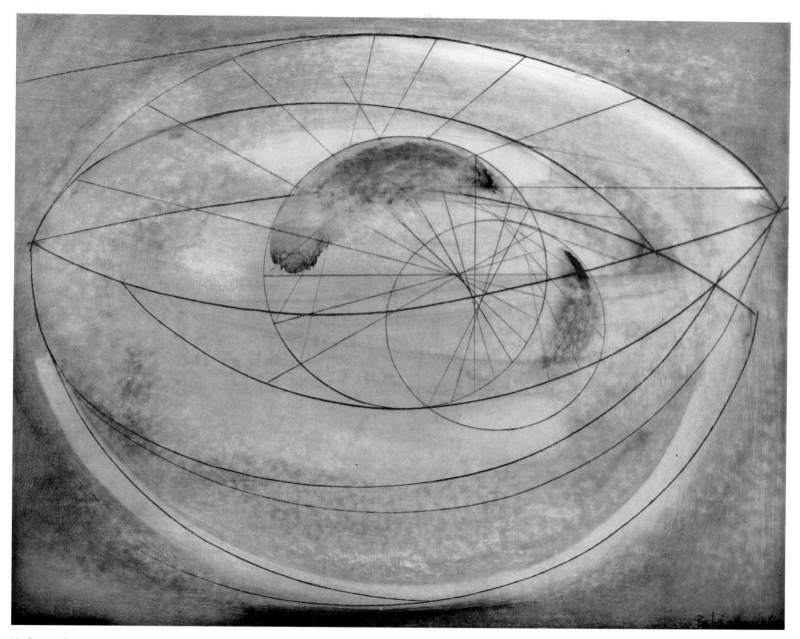

53 *Curved form on red*, 1962 (18 × 22 in.)

52 *Marble form (Mycenae)*, 1959 (20½ × 15½ in.)

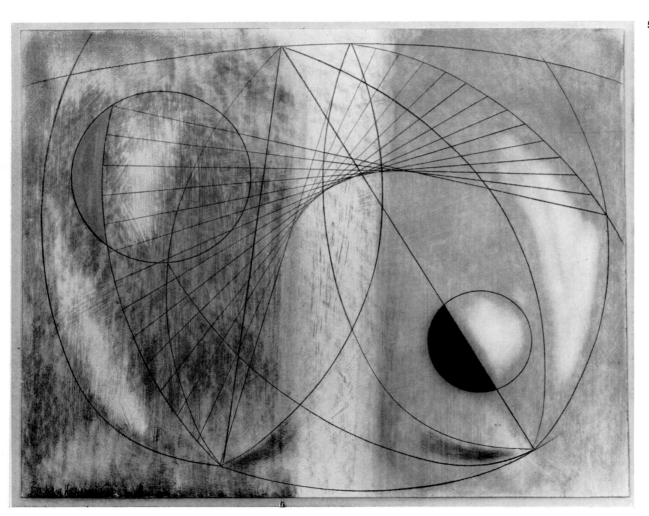

54 *Two forms,* 1963 (20 × 23¾ in.)

55 *Square and circle*, 1963 (36 × 18 in.)

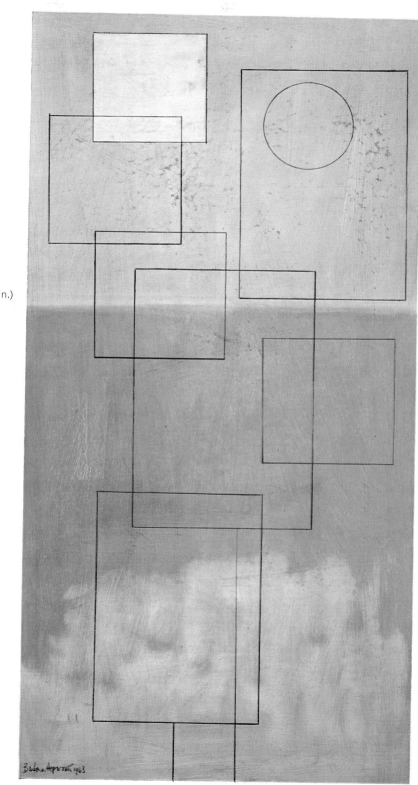

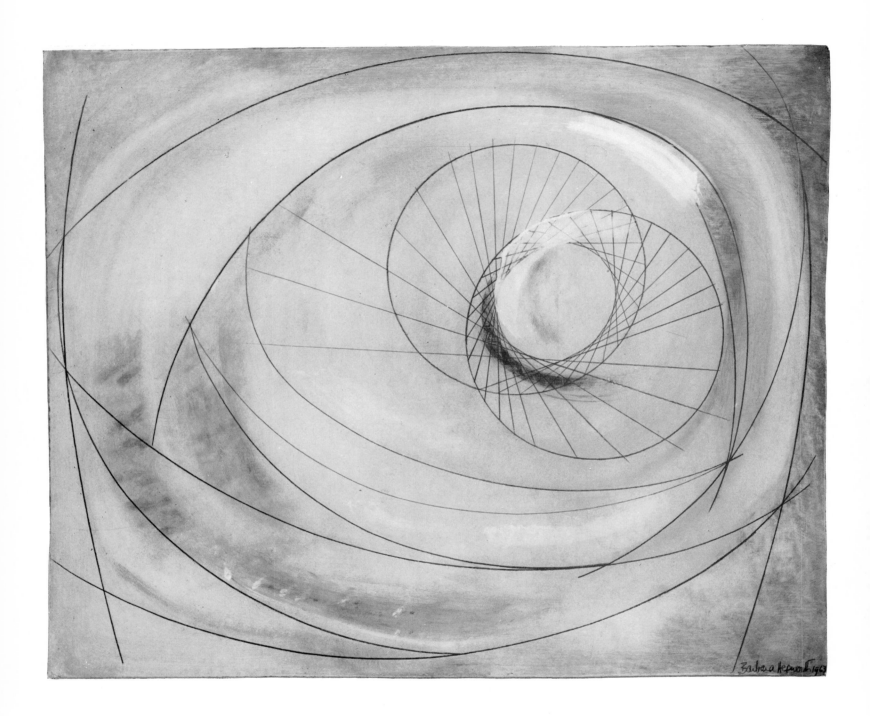

56 *Wave*, 1963 (19¾ × 23¾ in.)

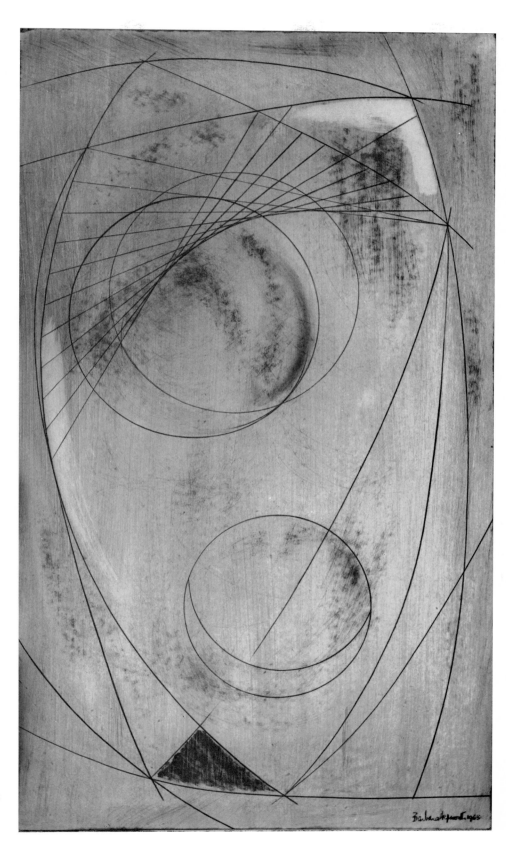

57 *Two circles*, 1963 (25 × 15 in.)

58 *Three monoliths*, 1964 (19 × 26 in.)

59 *Atlantic form* (*blue*), 1963 (25 × 18 in.)

60 *Square forms 2 (green and ochre)*, (36 × 18¼ in.)

61 *Goonhilly* (*September*), 1963 (18 × 24 in.)

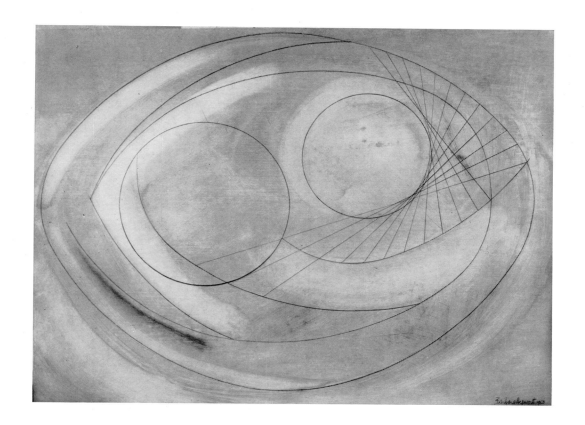

Barbara Hepworth

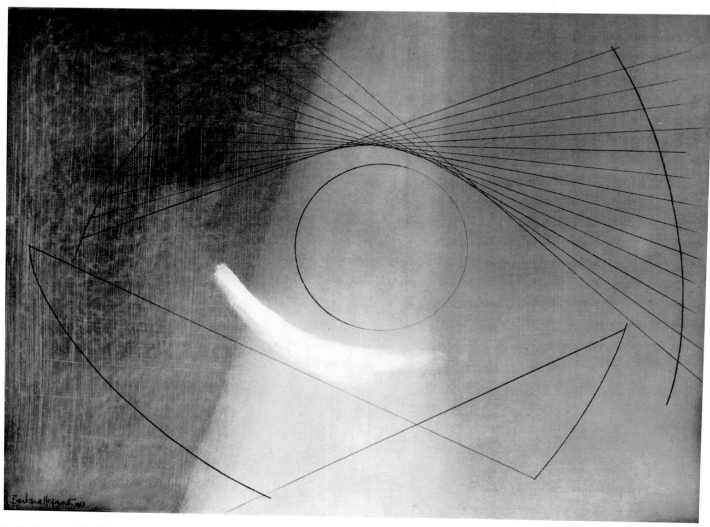

63 *Porthmeor*, 1963 (18 × 24 in.)

62 *Shell form*, 1963 (26 × 20 in.)

64 *Marble form*, 1964 (31¼ × 20¼ in.)

65 *Forms in echelon* (*green*), 1963 (15 × 26¾ in.)

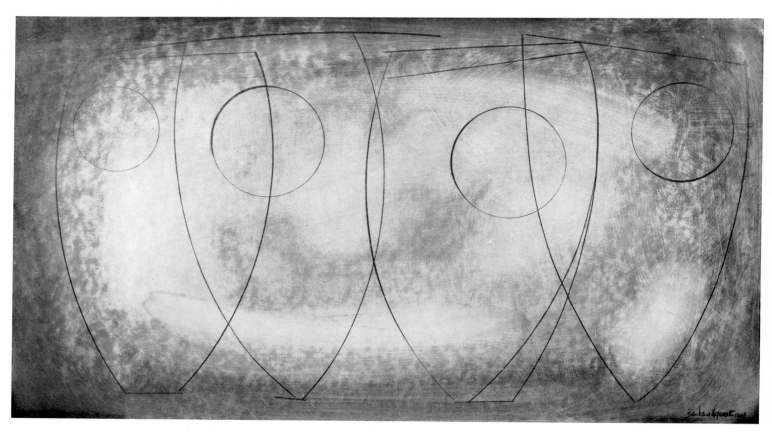

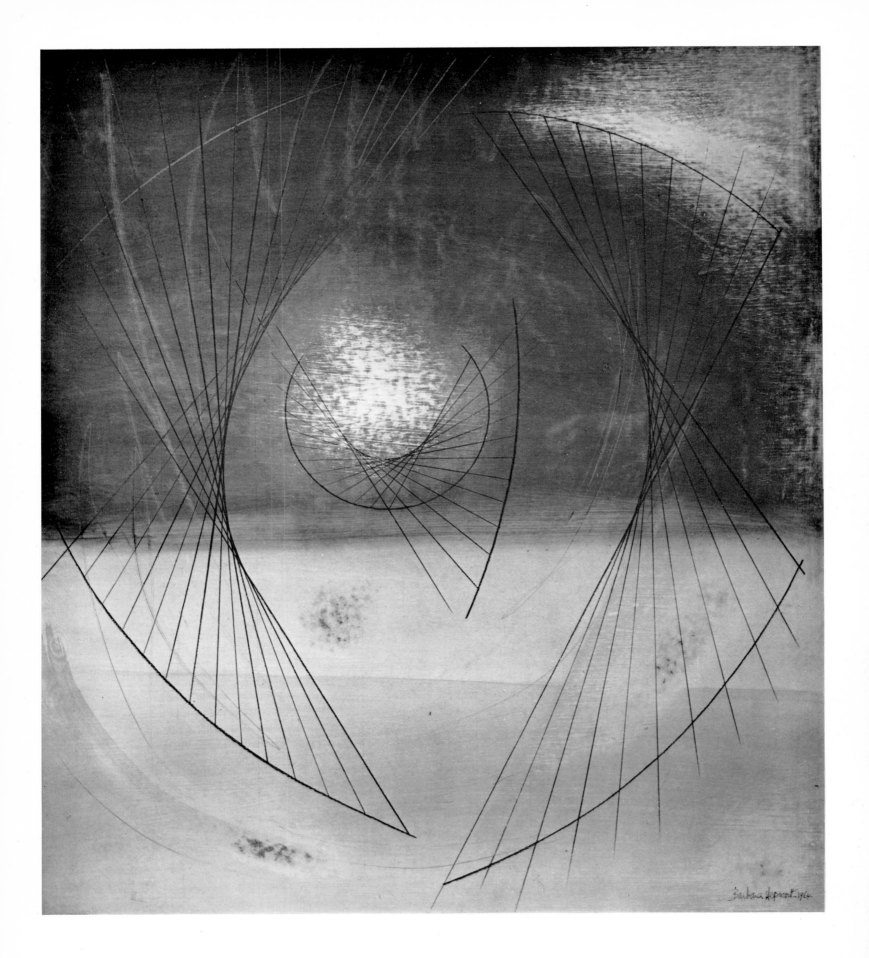

66 *Night sky (Porthmeor)*, 1964 (28 × 23¾ in.)

67 *Forms in echelon on an orange ground* (18 × 22 in.)

68 *Drawing for pierced form* (*May*), (30 × 40¾ in.)

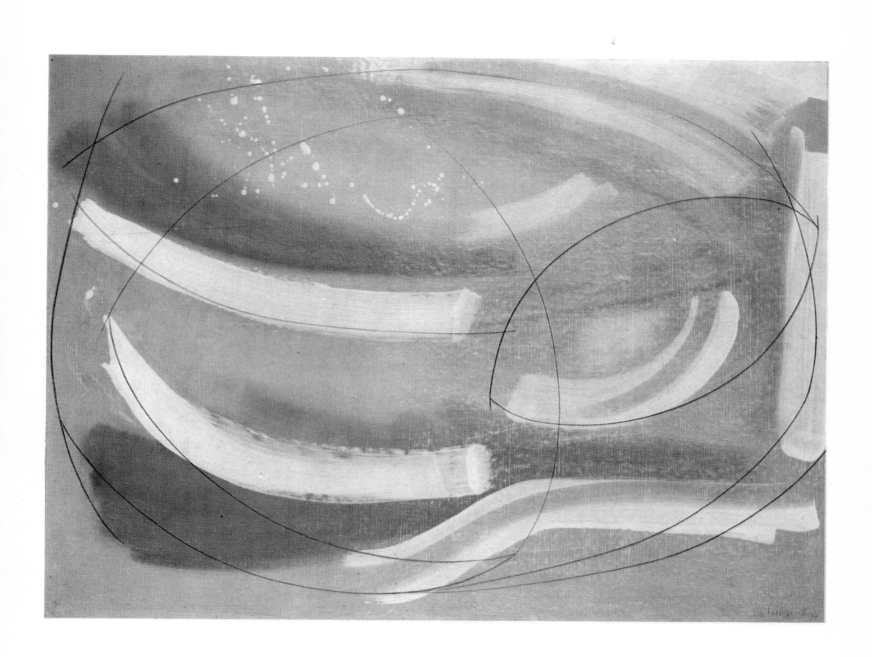

69 *Wave forms* (*Atlantic*), 1964 (30 × 40 in.)

70 *Construction I*, 1965 (35 × 40 in.)

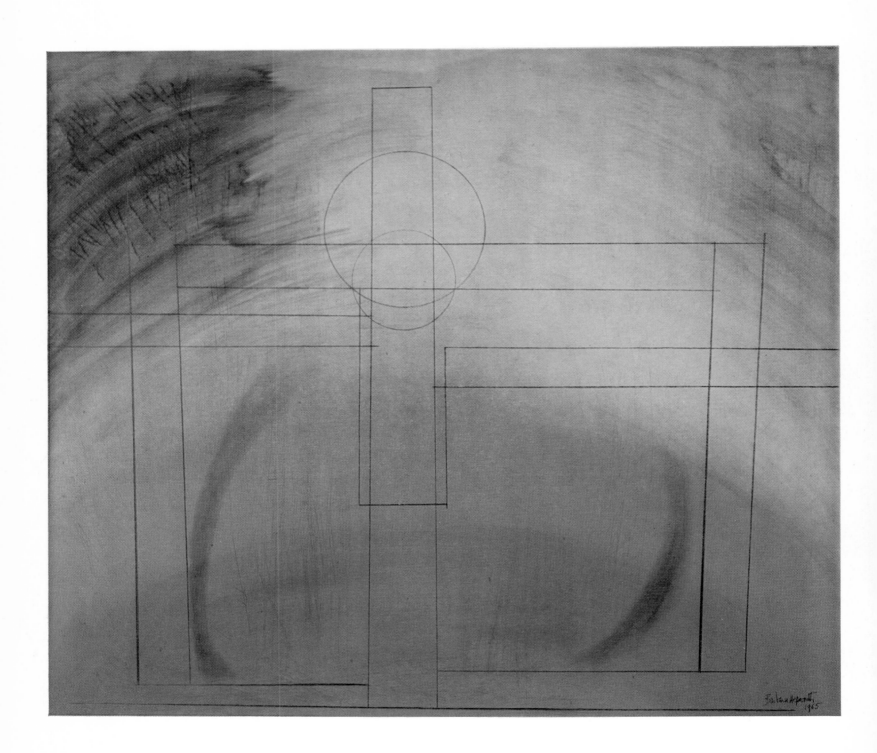

71 *Stringed figure*, 1965 (30 × 24 in.)

72 *Genesis II*, 1966 (26 × 26 in.)

73 *Wood form* (*Gothic*), 1966 (30 × 20 in.)

74 *Construction II*, 1966 (40 × 35 in.)

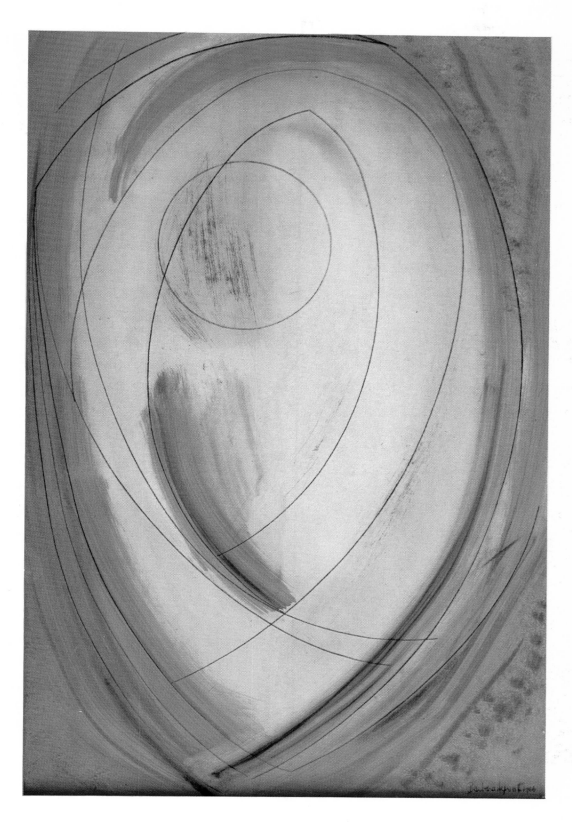

75 *Garden sculpture* (*marble*), 1966 (30 × 20 in.)

76 *Square form I*, 1966 (36 × 18 in.)